# 30 Day Keto Challenge

*The Official 30 Day Keto Guide to lose Rapid Weight, Burn Fat, and Transform your Lifestyle*

**Brandon Henry**

# Table of Contents

# Introduction

Welcome to your 30 days of Keto! By the end of this guide, you're going to have a 30-day plan that is as unique as you are! You'll be amazed at how easily you're able to transition to a state of ketosis when you throw out the idea of a cookie-cutter diet plan for one that you created yourself!

## What is the Keto Diet?

One of the reasons that many people are put off by the idea of the Keto Diet is because the science can seem a bit confusing. We're all too busy with our daily lives to be trying to figure out things like glucose and ketones and the perfect percentage of proteins and fats and carbs to help us lose weight.

And don't worry. In this guide, you're not going to get too bogged down by the biochemistry of the Keto Diet. In fact, I'm going to explain the process in the simplest of terms, not because I don't think you can understand the full complex picture, but instead so that you can focus on what's important - your 30-day diet.

The Keto Diet is based on the principle of ketosis. It's a process in which the body shifts from using carbohydrates to fat as its main source of energy. How exactly this works can be explained pretty simply. First, it's helpful to explain how your body breaks down food to give you energy. When you eat carbs, they are broken down into either glucose or glycogen - those are essentially just the scientific terms for simple sugars and complex sugars. Glucose is quick energy, and glycogen is tucked away for safe-keeping in case your glucose levels become low. And glucose can be stored as glycogen if you're not using it for energy right away. At the end of the day, it's all about how your body uses sugar to give you energy. So what happens when you stop eating so many carbs? Well, first, your body will dip into the glycogen reserves. But when that's low, it will start to burn ketones.

Wait, what are ketones? Well, when your body dips into your fat storage, it has to convert those fat molecules into something it can burn as energy. It's like if you were to go to the forest in search of firewood. You can't just pull a tree out of the ground. You've got to chop one down and then make it into small enough pieces to fit into your fireplace at home. Same idea here. Your body, without any glycogen, turns to your fat reserves for energy. Once it gets there, it turns that fat into ketones.

The great thing about the ketone is that it's a very strong source of energy. Whereas a simple sugar might give you a little kick, a ketone will burn brighter and last longer.

And that's the basic idea of the Keto Diet! Not so complicated, after all. Craving some more information? Let's move on.

# Why Do A 30 Day Challenge?

Some people choose to take the Keto Diet week by week or start out with a 14-day challenge. So why did you find yourself gravitating to a 30-day challenge instead?

There are a couple of benefits to jumping right into a month-long Keto challenge. The first is that you'll get a sense of how your body will change with Keto over time. When people try Keto for a week or two weeks, they may mistake short-term gains as a sign that they can ease up on the diet. Actually, it's very common to lose a surprising amount of weight in the first week due to a loss of water weight, but that doesn't mean that you've achieved full ketosis. So while a week-long challenge is a good start, it doesn't give you a true sense of what the Keto Diet can actually do for you.

There's another reason why it's helpful to take the 30-day challenge instead of a shorter option: endurance. When you're able to tackle a month-long challenge, it becomes much easier to keep the habit going. If you only stick to something for two weeks, it becomes much easier to think to yourself, That was so hard, I'm glad it's over. But when you achieve an entire month, you're more likely to think, Wow, I did that for an entire month. I could do it again. I know, you may have your doubts now, but trust me. You're not going to want to go back to your life before Keto if you've stuck to it for a month.

# Is This Diet Right For You?

As beneficial as the Keto Diet is for some folks, it's not the right diet for everyone. There are some people, such as people with Type 1 Diabetes, for whom it's dangerous to restrict the body's access to sugar as an energy source. Others may be discouraged because of thyroid or gallbladder issues.

As with any diet, it's important to talk to a doctor about any concerns you might have about starting your diet.

Generally, if you're in good health and are responsible about your nutrition, the Keto Diet will change your life for the better.

# How Can You Get Started?

Getting started on a 30-day Keto Diet is pretty simple. You're going to plan out your month with the most nutritious, healthy meals that you can. A good plan is the best way to start out a successful diet. And then, take it week-by-week, or day-by-day, or even meal-by-meal. See how your body feels. Adjust if you need to. Look for support. Build your inner strength.

What can you expect?

Everyone's body reacts a bit differently to the Keto Diet, but there are a few things that you can expect of the next 30 days.

First of all, it's important to consider that your body is going through a pretty significant change. There's going to be something of a transition period. This may manifest as a slight dip in energy and mental clarity, at first, before your body stabilizes. You might have some digestive fussiness, which is a sign that you should up your fiber intake. You'll likely be thirstier than usual, which is why it's going to be so important to drink plenty of fluids. For some people, these effects are similar to having the flu. For others, the transition isn't so severe. The important thing is to listen to your body and take care of yourself.

The good news is that the Keto Diet is known for its tendency to suppress appetite. What that means is that although you may find the diet a bit restrictive at first, over time, you won't feel cravings between meals. That's great news for anyone who has quit a diet because of the hunger pangs.

Another change that you'll experience early on is the water weight-loss. As your body burns through its stored glycogen, it's going to release some water. In the first week or two weeks, then, you're going to experience rapid weight-loss. Things will slow down after that, but don't worry. That doesn't mean that the diet isn't working anymore; it just means that you've tapped into your fat reserves and will start losing weight at a slower, steadier pace. That's perfectly healthy and normal.

By the end of your 30-day challenge, it would be very unusual if you didn't lose weight. In general, people lose significant amounts of weight when they switch to the Keto Diet, and how much you shed will depend on your exercise schedule and the recipes you chose for your 30-day plan.

In addition to the weight-loss, you'll find that you'll feel completely different by the end of the challenge. If you've stuck to your plan, your body has risen to the occasion - there should be no more grogginess, no more digestive issues, no more flu-like symptoms. You'll be so glad that you did the 30-day challenge and started your new Keto Diet lifestyle.

How can I help you?

This guide isn't meant to tell you exactly how to eat, when to eat, or what to eat. That would be really boring and ineffective. In reality, every person is different, with different tastes and different needs. You'll benefit more from a guide that helps you to figure out what is best for you to eat on your unique Keto journey.

The first chapter is brief, but it's going to help you get organized and make a plan that will truly work for you and your lifestyle. Some things that I'm going to ask you to consider are: your favorite foods, your access to ingredients, your personal schedule and responsibilities, and your tolerance for new things. This isn't to judge you, but rather to get you thinking about a 30-day challenge that is the most enjoyable for you. After all, you're changing your diet, but that doesn't mean that you have to be miserable. And with a good plan, you'll find that it's much easier than you might expect.

In the second chapter, you'll find recipes that you can use for your 30-day challenge. There are enough in the list for you to be able to choose the ones that sound tasty and overlook the ones that don't. You'll do some repeating of recipes over the month, but don't worry. The collection of recipes is unique enough to keep you engaged and diverse enough to give you nutritional variety.

Chapter Three offers up a 30-day Keto Diet template, but again, it's important that you create your own. If it does look inviting to you, integrate it into your lifestyle the way that makes the most sense to you.

I'm so excited to be guiding you through this wonderful challenge. So without any more introductions, let's jump right in!

# Chapter One: Set Yourself Up for Success

I've often seen people jump into a diet the moment that they buy their first guide book. And for some people, that works. But for the vast majority of us, it's important to have a plan in place before we start something like the Keto Diet. This chapter will help you create a foolproof plan for your month of Keto.

Each of the follow sections are tasks that you're going to want to complete before you start your diet. I know the tendency to get started now that you're feeling inspired, but take the pause to consider these suggestions. They'll help make your plan more accessible.

## The Keto Calendar

The very first thing you'll need for your month-long challenge is a blank calendar. You can also use an app. Just make sure you're able to include both your everyday responsibilities, your exercise schedule, and your meals. That's a lot of information, so you'll need plenty of space to see everything laid out. It's also helpful, if you're physically writing your calendar, to use pencil or have no problem with white-out. Things change, and you want your calendar to be flexible.

Some people find it helpful also to include daily or weekly logs. This is simply a space for you to write down how you're feeling, any challenges that you might have had, and any successes.

## Find Your Keto Breakdown

You've probably heard about low-fat, low-carb, or high-protein diets, which are all considered macro diets. Usually, people on these diets want to lose weight or build muscle or reach their fitness goals. The Keto Diet is a bit different. You don't actually have to count calories if you don't want to. In fact, by cutting out carbs from your diet, you will naturally eat less calories per day than ever before. However, I've seen many people on Keto who, because they're not paying much attention to the nutrition facts, end up eating carbs without even realizing it. Fruits and vegetables, for instance, can be full of carbs, but you would never know if you didn't take the time to look at the nutrition facts.

So, for the purposes of a 30-day challenge, I think it's still helpful to be aware of how many calories you're consuming and how many are coming from fat, protein, and carbs. This will help you to reach ketosis as quickly as possible, and it will also allow you to be more comfortable with which ingredients are safe for your Keto Diet even after the 30 days.

Here, we're going to be following the standard Keto macro breakdown: 60% fat, 30% protein, and 10% carbs. What does that mean? It means that of your daily allotment of calories, 60% will come from fat, 30% from protein, and, well, you get the point. There are different versions of this breakdown - some of the more intense options suggest no more than 5% carbs, and some range between 60% and 80% for fats, and 15% and 35% for protein.

The reason why we're going with the 60/30/10 standard here is because it is the most accessible while also being highly effective. If you want to push yourself to eating no more than 5% carbs per day, by all means, go for it! But for many of us, especially if we've never limited our carb intake before, a percentage that low will only result in burnout and frustration with the diet. Our chances of success, in other words, are simply higher with a more manageable ratio.

Okay, so how can you know how many grams of protein, fat, and carbs you'll need, specifically? You can easily find your daily calories by plugging in your information into an online calculator, or you can simply follow the recommended daily calorie intake for your weight and activity level. Here's a breakdown.

According to experts, a man between the ages of 21 and 40 should be consuming somewhere between 2400 and 2800 calories per day depending on how active he is. If he's very active, that number may increase to 3000 calories per day.

Women in the same age bracket should be eating between 1800 and 2200 depending on her activity levels. Very active women can eat up to 2400 calories per day.

And, you don't have to overthink this. If you are a 30-year-old woman with an office job who exercises moderately every day, you might set a goal for yourself to eat 2100 calories per day. If you are a 26-year-old male who doesn't exercise at all, you might eat somewhere around 2400 calories per day. Whatever daily calorie intake number you choose, as long as it's within a reasonable range for your age and activity level, the Keto Diet will help you to burn fat. Simple.

Great, so now that you have your daily calorie intake, you can use the Standard Keto Calculation to figure out how many calories per day are coming from fat, protein, and carbs.

Let's start with fat. You want 60% of your calories to come from fat. That means if you eat 2000 calories per day, 1200 of those calories will come from fat. Now, if you wanted to convert that into grams, which is helpful because most recipes are written in grams, you would divide that number by 9 (Why 9? There are 9 grams of fat in every calorie we consume). You get about 133.3g of fat per day

Let's do the same calculation for protein. For a diet with 2000 calories, you would eat 600 calories of protein. That number, to convert to grams, would be divided by 4, which gives you 150g per day of protein.

And finally, the smallest number in your daily roundup, the carbs. Only 10% of your daily calories will come from carbs, which gives you 200 calories, or when divided by 4, 50g of carbs per day.

Here's a simple breakdown of the math so that you can do it for your unique calorie intake:

Fat: .60 multiplied by your daily calorie intake, divided by 9

Protein: .30 multiplied by your daily calorie intake, divided by 4

Carbs: .10 multiplied by your daily calorie intake, divided by 4

Once you have your daily breakdown figured out, it will be much easier to choose your meals for the day and know that you're on track to achieve ketosis and lose weight.

Now, I know that all sounded like very exact math, and it's tempting to feel bound by those numbers. But, again, that's not what the Keto Diet is about. Many people on the Keto Diet don't count calories at all. These equations, instead, are meant to be helpful so that you have an idea of your calorie breakdown, especially when it comes to carbs. So, if you're the kind of person who enjoys counting calories, then you might rely more on these equations. If you don't consider yourself a very mathematically-inclined individual, maybe you just focus on your carb intake, or drop the equations altogether.

Consider Intermittent Fasting

Every day, science is finding a new benefit to occasional fasting for everything from the obvious weight-loss to the more surprising outcomes like slower aging and improved brain function. When it comes to the Keto Diet, many argue that intermittent fasting decreases the time that it takes to achieve ketosis, which means that you'll breeze through the negative symptoms faster while burning fat.

If you choose to incorporate intermittent fasting in your 30-day Keto challenge, there are a couple of different routes you can take. The most popular is the 16:8 fast, in which you eat during an 8 hour window, and fast for the rest of the time. That means that you might have a meal at 9am, 12pm, and 5pm and then eat nothing until the next morning. Most of that time is spent sleeping, so this is a very accessible option for many people.

Another option might be to schedule a 24-hour fast once a week or every other day. This, obviously, ranges in difficulty, so you should choose which option is going to be most successful for you.

Finally, there's the option of one or two meals per day. Maybe you have one giant meal around lunch time that has all of your calories for the day. Maybe you eat breakfast and lunch, and then skip dinner.

The most important thing here is that you're strategic with your planning. Don't schedule a fast on the day that you have to give a big presentation at work. Perhaps you can also look at the weather and decide not to fast on a day that you're going to be out in the sun and are putting yourself at risk for heat exhaustion. Again, a calendar is a great tool for deciding when you should fast.

Also, if you're thinking of fasting as part of your 30-day Keto Challenge, you'll want to decide when to start. Some people feel that ketosis can be more quickly achieved when you incorporate fasting early on. Others suggest that you wait to reach ketosis before introducing fasting as part of your diet. The science hasn't been released to say definitively which is better, so it's more a matter of personal preference at this point. If you feel like eating a low-carb diet is going to be challenging enough without also dealing with fasting, wait until you've reached ketosis so that the hunger suppression will work in your favor. If you'd rather jump right in, then you can start fasting right away.

And one last thing about fasting - if you decide to fast, make sure to listen to your body and adjust if necessary. Some fatigue and lightheadedness is normal, but extreme exhaustion or fainting is not.

## The Hydration Plan

Yes, the Keto Diet is all about what you're eating, but staying hydrated is really important. There are quite a few reasons why drinking water on Keto is so crucial to your overall health. On the one hand, you're going to be taking out some fundamental sources of water such as fruits and root crops from your diet. Also, your body is going to need extra water to be able to help stabilize the digestive process when you might be struggling to get enough fiber. Because every person is different, I'm not going to tell you how much to drink. But when you're planning out your 30-day Keto Challenge, it might be a good idea to buy yourself a nice, new water bottle to encourage yourself to always have water available.
Or, you might add a daily water goal to your calendar, so that you can track how much you're actually drinking and adjust if needed.

## Create a Support System

Finally, the best thing that you can do when you're putting together your 30-day Keto Diet challenge is to find a good support system. Change can be difficult, both mentally and physically, but it's much easier when the people around you are supportive and helpful. Obviously, you can't expect everyone in your life to suddenly jump on the Keto bandwagon, but you should try to find one or two people who can help you throughout the month. And what do I mean by help? Well, if you have a friend who is willing to do the 30-day challenge with you, great! Or, help can be something as small as listening to you without judgment when you need someone to complain to. Because the Keto diet is a relatively new phenomenon in the health community, not everyone is going to be supportive of your decision or understand why you chose this path. But if you can find a few people to give you positive energy during the month, make sure to take advantage!

And hey, if you don't have anyone in your life who will act as that support system, turn to your local health community or online. There are so many people out there benefiting from the Keto Diet; you just have to find them.

You're just about ready!

At this point, you have all of the resources to get started on your 30-day Keto Diet Challenge, except, of course, the actual plan. But before we turn to the recipes, do one last check to see if you have everything else organized:

A calendar that, at this point, is filled in with your daily tasks and exercise schedule. Make sure there's enough space to add your meals.

Your daily calorie intake broken down into grams of fat, protein, and carbs. Remember, the recommended Keto breakdown is 60% fat, 30% protein, and 10% carbs.

Scheduled fasting. Remember, this is optional, but if you decide to fast, make sure that you include it in your calendar.

A hydration plan to make sure that you always have water accessible. Dehydration is common, so have a plan to reduce your risk!

Your support system. This can be people in your life who are there to give you encouragement. And, remember, there's an entire community of Keto-enthusiasts out there, so make connections!

You're ready to put together you 30-day challenge!

# Chapter Two: Mapping Your Thirty Days

In this chapter, you're going to be able to choose all of the recipes that you can include on your 30-day Keto Diet. It's broken into four sections: breakfast, lunch, dinner, and snacks, but remember - everything will depend on your daily calorie intake and your fasting schedule. Some days you might choose to have two high-calorie meals. Other days, you might choose to have four small-portioned meals. It's all up to your preferences.

You'll find 10 breakfast recipes, 15 lunch recipes, 15 dinner recipes and 10 snack options. The reason why I haven't included 30 recipes in each sections is because you're actually going to be grateful to cycle through the same meal once or twice. Sticking to a Keto Diet for a month is challenging enough without having to become a diversified and talented chef. Instead, it will be much easier to be able to choose 5 to 10 recipes in each category and learn how to make them quickly and well. And don't worry, the recipes are unique enough that you won't feel like you're eating the same boring meal of cooked chicken and zucchini every day.

As you go through these recipes, take note of the ones that you would like to try and then pencil them into your calendar. Take into consideration that you might have more time to make a more complicated recipe on your day off from work or that you'll want the quick and easy recipes on the days that you're really busy.

## One Thing to Remember: Access to Ingredients

Another important thing to consider as you create your 30-day Keto challenge is your access to ingredients. If you are taking on this diet in the middle of winter, it might not be a great idea to pull recipes that feature vegetables only available in the summer. Or, if you live in a small, rural town, it might be more difficult to get specially items. I've done my best to include delicious recipes that don't ask you to do too much searching anyway, but some ingredients just aren't easily available everywhere.

Of course, you can substitute ingredients to make things a bit easier, but remember to adjust your other meals if necessary so as not to go over your daily calorie allotment.

You can stray, but consider this

All of the recipes in this chapter feature 100% Keto-approved ingredients. If you follow these recipes, you'll know that you're on a Keto Diet. However, if you'd like to stray, you're more than welcome to do so. Including other ingredients that you like more will allow you to take ownership over your 30-day challenge and keep you more engaged. Just remember, not all that seems Keto is, so steer clear of these ingredients:

All grains, including oats, rice, corn, and quinoa

All fruits except low-carb berries like strawberries, blueberries, raspberries, and blackberries

Legumes, including peanuts

High-carb vegetables like potatoes, carrots, parsnips, and sweet potatoes. Basically, if it grows underground, chances are, it's a high-carb vegetable

All sugars, even honey, maple syrup, agave, and especially white sugar or high-fructose corn syrup

When in doubt, look at the carb content.

# Breakfast Recipes

## Eggs and Bacon

Ingredients:

- 2 medium eggs
- 2 slices of bacon
- Pepper

Nutrition breakdown:

331 calories, 24.6g of fat, 25.2g of protein, 1.2g of carbs

This recipe is so aligned with the perfect Keto breakdown that if you're happy with it, you can have it for breakfast every morning.

## Cheesy Scrambled Eggs

Ingredients:

- 2 medium eggs
- 2 tablespoons of filtered water
- 1/2 cup of your favorite cheese
- Salt and pepper

Instructions. In a medium bowl, whisk together the eggs and water. Add the cheese, salt and pepper. Cook over medium heat, stirring occasionally, to your liking.

Nutrition breakdown:

394 calories, 30.7g of fat, 26.9g of protein, 1.5g of carbs

# Mushroom and Spinach Omelet

Ingredients:

- 3 eggs
- 2 tablespoons of water
- 1/2 cup of white mushrooms, sliced
- 1 cup of spinach
- 1/2 cup of your favorite cheese
- Salt and pepper

Instructions:

I like to sauté the mushrooms and spinach in a little bit of butter before adding to the omelet, but that step is optional.

To make the omelet, whisk together the eggs, water, salt and pepper. Pour into a medium-sized pan (not too big or the omelet will come out too thin.) When the egg begins to cook, you'll be able to lift up the edges and allow the liquid on top to flow underneath. Flip the omelet and add the filling to half of the omelet, topped with cheese.

Cook for one minute more and then serve by folding the omelet in half over the filling.

Nutrition breakdown:
471 calories, 35.1g of fat, 34.4g of protein, 4.1g of carbs

## Scrambled Eggs and Lox

Ingredients:
- 2 medium eggs
- 6 ounces of lox (smoked salmon), cut into bite-sized slices
- 1 tablespoon of water
- 1/2 of a stalk of green onion
- Salt and Pepper

Instructions:
Whisk the eggs, water, salt and pepper. Cook over medium heat, stirring every few minutes. When the eggs are almost done to your liking, add the salmon. Remove from heat and serve with chopped green onions on top.

Nutrition breakdown:
389 calories, 19.9g of fat, 47.7g of protein, 1.29g of carbs

# Avocado Egg Bake

Ingredients:

- 2 small eggs
- 1 avocado, cut in half and pit removed
- 1/8 of a cup of cheese for topping
- (optional) 1 slice of bacon, cooked and crumbled
- Salt and Pepper

Instructions:

Preheat the oven to 375 degrees. Place the avocados skin side down on a baking sheet. Scoop out a bit of the inside - enough for the egg to snuggle in. Bake for about 20 minutes, or until the egg is done to your liking. Top with the salt, pepper and cheese and optional bacon. Put it back in the oven just for a minute or two to melt the cheese.

Nutrition breakdown:

With bacon: 623 calories, 53.9g of fat, 22.5g of protein, 18.2g of carbs

Without the bacon: 517 calories, 43.7g of fat, 19.2g of protein, 18g of carbs

# Berry Smoothie

Ingredients:

- 1/8 cup of strawberries
- 1/8 cup of blueberries
- 1/2 cup of spinach
- 1/2 cup of water
- 1/2 cup of coconut milk (you can substitute almond milk or cashew milk)

Instructions:

Blend everything together for a filling, refreshing morning smoothie!

Nutrition breakdown:

With coconut milk: 261 calories, 24.3g of fat, 3.1g of protein, 12.5g of carbs

## Cherry Chia Bowl

- 1/8 cup cherries, pitted
- 1/8 cup of strawberries
- 1/4 cup of coconut milk
- 2 tablespoons of chia seeds

Instructions:

In a bowl or mason jar, mix all ingredients. Allow to sit at room temperature for about 10 minutes. Stir and put it in the fridge overnight. The consistency should be thick, like pudding.

Nutrition breakdown:

268 calories, 20.9g of fat, 6.2g of protein, 18.2g of carbs

# Keto Toast

Ingredients:

- 1 and a half cups almond flour (you can add a bit more if you feel that your dough is sticky)
- 1/2 teaspoon ground flax seed
- 1 teaspoon baking powder
- 1/2 cup of unsalted butter, at room temperature
- 6 eggs, at room temperature
- 1 tablespoon of coconut oil
- 1 teaspoon of salt
- 1 teaspoon of dried herbs like thyme, oregano, rosemary, etc. (optional)

Instructions:

Preheat the oven to 350 degrees. In a large mixing bowl, beat the eggs until light, about 2 to 3 minutes (5 minutes if you're hand mixing.) Mix in the butter and coconut oil.

In a separate bowl, mix the flour, baking powder, flax seed, salt and herbs. Slowly add the dry ingredients into the wet ingredients, while blending.

In a greased bread pan, pour in the mixture. Bake for about 40 to 50 minutes, or until a toothpick comes out clean.

This recipe makes about 8 thick slices of bread. Now, you can toast and serve with low-car jam or butter.

Nutrition breakdown:

Per slice:

103 calories, 9.9g of fat, 3.3g of protein, .5g of carbs

# Keto Eggy Bread

Ingredients:

- 2 slices of Keto bread
- 2 eggs
- 1 tablespoon butter
- 1/8 cup of heavy whipping cream
- Dusting of cinnamon
- Dusting of nutmeg

- 1/8 cup of strawberries

Instructions:

In a shallow bowl, mix the eggs and heavy whipping cream. Dip the slices of Keto bread in the mixture and place in a medium-size pan with butter over medium heat.

Sprinkle with the cinnamon and nutmeg, and serve with strawberries.

Nutrition breakdown:

627 calories, 56.4g of fat, 25.1g of protein, 4.9g of carbs

# Fresh-Pressed Green Juice

- 2 stalks of celery
- 1 cup of spinach
- 1/2 cucumber
- 1" of ginger
- 1 cup of water

Instructions:

In your juicer, juice the celery, spinach, cucumber and ginger and mix with water.

Nutrition breakdown:

27 calories, .4g of fat, 1.7g of protein, 4.8g of carbs

# Lunch Recipes

Before we get into the actual recipes, a quick note on lunches. Of all the meals that you're going to eat during the day, this one is the trickiest. If you work in an office, or you're out and about during the day, the temptation to buy something or grab lunch with friends is going to be very high. That's why you should take extra consideration about your lunches. Choose recipes that you know you'll like and that you won't mind cooking for yourself in advance. I also recommend that once or twice a week, you choose a dinner recipe that will easily give you leftovers so that you don't have to do any extra work.

And remember, lunch doesn't have to be complicated. Just choose the recipes that sound tasty and will be simple to make.

## Keto Meatballs

Ingredients:
- 1/2 pound of ground turkey
- 1/2 pound of ground pork
- 1 egg
- 1/8 cup of fresh parsley

- 2 cloves garlic, minced and mashed
- 1/2 onion, chopped and mashed
- 1/2 teaspoon each of salt, pepper, and oregano
- 1/8 cup of parmesan
- 1/4 cup heavy cream

Instructions:

Preheat the oven to 375 degrees.

In a large mixing bowl, add all ingredients and mix well. Don't be afraid to use your hands to make sure you have a smooth, well-combined mixture. Roll meatballs in your palms until you get 12 of the same size. You can also make smaller ones.

Bake on a lined or greased baking sheet for about 20 to 25 minutes.

Nutrition breakdown:

For 6 meatballs:

702 calories, 43.3g of fat, 66.3g of protein, 10.1g of carbs

# Garlic Shrimp

Ingredients:
- 1/2 pound of shrimp, peeled and deveined
- 1/4 cup of butter
- 3 cloves of garlic
- 1/8 cup of fresh parsley

- Juice of 1/2 to a whole lemon
- Salt and pepper

Instructions:

In a medium-sized pan, heat the butter and garlic until fragrant. Add in the shrimp and cook until pink. Mix in the parsley, lemon juice, salt and pepper. Remove from heat, and serve hot.

Nutrition breakdown:

622 calories, 47.4g of fat, 47g of protein, 5.2g of carbs

# Cobb Salad

Ingredients:
- 1 small chicken breast, cooked
- 1 head of your favorite lettuce, cut into ribbons
- 1/2 cup cherry tomatoes, halved
- 1 egg, hard-boiled
- 1/2 avocado
- 1 slice of bacon, cooked and crumbled
- 1/8 cup of crumbled blue cheese
- Salt and pepper, to taste

For the dressing:
- 4 tablespoons of olive oil

- 1 tablespoon of Dijon mustard
- 4 tablespoons of red wine vinegar
- Juice of one lemon

Instructions:

In a large bowl, mix all salad ingredients. In a small measuring bowl or mason jar, whisk together dressing ingredients.

As you're preparing this for lunch, keep the dressing separate from the salad until serving. This recipe makes two big servings of salad.

Nutrition breakdown:

One serving: 626 calories, 47.8g of fat, 37.1g of protein, 13.6g of carbs

# Brussels Sprouts and Kale Salad with Ranch Dressing

Ingredients:

For the salad:

- 1 cup of Brussels sprouts, shredded
- 1 cup of kale, cut in ribbons (it helps to crunch them in your hands some to break down the fibers and release some of the bitterness)
- 1/8 cup of pecans
- 1/8 cup of dried cranberries

- 1 slice of bacon, cooked and crumbled
- 1/8 cup of crumbled feta cheese (or blue cheese)

For the dressing:
- 1/4 cup of sour cream (you can use cream cheese for a subtler taste)
- 1/4 cup of mayonnaise
- 1/8 cup of whole milk or heavy whipping cream
- 1 garlic clove, minced
- 3 chives, minced
- Juice from half a lemon
- 1 teaspoon each of dried parsley, dill, and onion powder
- Salt and pepper

Instructions:

In a large bowl, combine all salad ingredients. In a separate measuring bowl or mason jar, whisk together all dressing ingredients.

Again, if you're preparing this for lunch, keep the dressing separate from the salad until serving. This recipe makes two big servings of salad.

Nutrition breakdown:

Per serving: 326 calories, 25.3g of fat, 8.9g of protein, 18.9g of carbs

# Mediterranean Salad

Ingredients:

- 1 cucumber, cut into quarters
- 1 small red onion, chopped
- 1 cup of cherry tomatoes, halved
- 1/2 yellow bell pepper
- 1/2 cup of olives (your favorite)
- 2 tablespoons of crumbled feta
- 1/8 cup of fresh parsley, chopped
- 1/8 cup of fresh mint, chopped (optional)
- For the dressing:
- 2 tablespoons of olive oil
- Juice from half a lemon
- 1 clove of garlic
- Salt and pepper


Instructions:

Allow the tomatoes to sit in salt for about 15 minutes to soak up some of the liquid. Then, combine all salad ingredients in a large mixing bowl. Mix the dressing ingredients separately and drizzle over the salad. Because the salad ingredients aren't as susceptible to becoming soggy, it's not a big deal to pour the dressing ingredients over the salad in the morning instead of taking two separate containers.

This recipe makes 2 servings.

Nutrition breakdown:

For one serving: 660 calories, 54g of fat, 26.7g of protein, 20.7g of carbs

Now, this recipe, while delicious and full of healthy fats, is also high in carbs. Make sure to pair it with a breakfast and dinner that is low in carbs or work it into your fasting schedule.

# Chicken and Broccoli

Ingredients:

- 1/2 pound of chicken, cut into bite-sized pieces
- 1/2 head of broccoli, chopped into bite-sized pieces
- 2 cloves of garlic
- 2 green onions, chopped
- 1 teaspoon sesame oil
- 1 tablespoon olive oil
- 1/4 cup of coconut aminos (not absolutely necessary, but it's a good replacement for soy sauce, which is higher in carbs. If you can't find coconut aminos, you can use 4 tablespoons of soy sauce)
- 1/2 teaspoon red pepper flakes
- Salt and pepper to taste

Instructions:

In a medium-sized pan, heat the olive oil and garlic. When fragrant, add the chicken pieces and cook through. Remove the chicken from the pan with a slotted spoon and set aside. In the same pan, cook the broccoli with a few tablespoons of water, covered, for five minutes or until the broccoli is close to done. Remove the lid and cook off the excess water.

Add the chicken back to the pan with the sesame oil, salt, pepper, red pepper flakes, and coconut aminos/soy sauce. Mix well and serve with green onions as a garnish.

Nutrition breakdown:

With soy sauce: 522 calories, 25.2g of fat, 57.6g of protein, 18g of carbs

# Beef and Cauliflower Rice

Ingredients:

For the beef:

- 1/2 pound of beef chuck, cut into bite-sized pieces
- 2 cloves of garlic, minced
- 1 bay leaf
- 1 cup of beef broth
- Half of a green or red bell pepper, chopped
- 1/2 yellow onion
- 1 teaspoon each of salt, pepper, thyme, and oregano

- 1 tablespoon of almond flour, as a thickening agent
- 1 tablespoon of olive oil

For the cauliflower rice:
- 1/2 head of cauliflower, shredded
- 1/2 tablespoon olive oil

Instructions:

In a medium stock pot, heat olive oil over medium heat. Add the garlic and pieces of beef. Brown the beef on all sides and then add the onion and bell pepper. Cook until the bell pepper and onion are translucent. Add the seasonings and beef broth. Cover and cook until the beef is completely cooked and flakes easily. It should take about 45 minutes. If you want the broth to be thicker, add in the almond flour.

To make the cauliflower rice, heat the oil in a medium sauce pan and add cauliflower. Cook until it reaches the consistency you want for your rice. You can also cover for a sticker texture.

Serve the beef stew over the rice. This recipe makes 2 servings.

Nutrition breakdown:

470 calories, 33.6g of fat, 31.3g of protein, 15.8g of carbs

# Super Green Loaded Salad with Raspberry Vinaigrette

Ingredients:

- 1/2 cup spinach
- 1/2 cup arugula or dandelion greens
- 1/2 cup of red lettuce
- 1/2 onion, chopped
- 1 tomato, chopped
- 1/8 cup of walnuts
- 2 tablespoons sunflower seeds
- 1/2 cucumber, cut in rounds
- 1 green onion, chopped
- 1 handful cilantro or parsley
- Salt and pepper

For the dressing:

- 1/4 cup of olive oil
- 6 ounces of fresh raspberries
- 1/2 tablespoon of red wine vinegar
- 1/2 tablespoon of apple cider vinegar
- 1 teaspoon Dijon mustard
- Salt and pepper

Instructions:

Mix together all salad ingredients. In a separate measuring cup or mason jar, mix together dressing ingredients. Keep separate until serving.

This recipe makes 2 to 3 servings of salad.

Nutrition breakdown:

Per bowl: 325 calories, 26.6g of fat, 6.1g of protein, 20.5g of carbs

# Keto Tuna on Cucumber Chips

Ingredients:

- 1 small can of tuna, in water, drained
- 1 to 2 tablespoons of mayonnaise
- 1 teaspoon Dijon mustard
- 1/4 onion, chopped
- Salt and pepper
- 1/2 of a cucumber, cut into rounds

Instructions:

In a medium-sized mixing bowl, combine the tuna, mayonnaise, mustard, onion, salt and pepper with a fork. Serve on the cucumber rounds.

Nutrition breakdown:

272 calories, 12.3g of fat, 33.7g of protein, 8.4g of carbs

# Cauliflower Soup

Ingredients:

- 1 head of cauliflower, cut into small pieces
- 1 tablespoon of avocado or olive oil
- 1 tablespoon butter, unsalted
- 1 teaspoon each of salt, pepper, onion powder, and cayenne pepper
- 1/2 yellow onion, chopped
- 1 stalk of celery
- 2 cloves of garlic, minced
- 2 cups of chicken broth
- 1/2 cup of heavy whipping cream
- 4 tablespoons of cream cheese
- 1 and 1/2 cup of your favorite cheese

Instructions:

Preheat the oven to 350 degrees. On a greased cookie sheet, place the cauliflower in a single layer. Cover with a tablespoon of olive oil, salt and pepper. Bake for about 25 minutes.

While the cauliflower is roasting, melt the butter in a medium- to large-sized stock pot. Add in the garlic, onions, and celery and cook until translucent and very soft. Add in the cauliflower and cook for another one to two minutes. Add the chicken broth along with 1/2 cup of water. Bring everything to a boil and then lower the heat to simmer and cover. Cook the soup for about 20 minutes.

With a hand-held soup blender, blend all ingredients together. You can also transfer the soup to a standing blender or use a potato masher. Stir in the dairy items until everything is well mixed.

This recipe makes 3 to 4 bowls of soup.

Nutrition breakdown:

Per serving when divided into four portions: 394 calories, 34.5g of fat, 15.6g of protein, 6.9g of carbs

# Cream of Celery Soup

Ingredients:

- 1 bunch of celery, about 7 to 10 stalks
- 2 yellow onions, chopped
- 5 cloves of garlic
- 3 and 1/2 cups of chicken stock
- 1/2 cup heavy cream (or more if you want it to be creamier)
- 2 bay leaves
- 3 tablespoons of unsalted butter
- 1 teaspoon dried parsley
- 3 chives, chopped

- Salt and pepper, to taste
- 1 teaspoon of xanthan gum or 1 tablespoon of almond flour for thickness (optional)

Instructions:

In a medium- to large-sized stock pot, heat the butter over medium heat. Add the garlic and cook until fragrant. Add the onions and the celery. Cook until all ingredients are very soft, about 20 minutes. If the pot starts to become dry, add a bit of the chicken broth to add moisture.

After about 20 minutes, add the stock, bay leaves, parsley, salt and pepper. Bring the soup to boil and then turn down the heat and simmer for another 20 to 30 minutes.

Add the cream and the thickening agent if you're using one. With a hand-held blender, you can blend the soup in the pot. Otherwise, transfer to a standing blender or use a potato masher to get the consistency you want. Serve with chives as a garnish.

This recipe makes about 5 bowls of soup.

Nutrition breakdown:

Per serving: 150 calories, 13.3g of fat, 2.4g of protein, 6.1g of carbs

# Pesto Chicken

Ingredients:
- 1/2 pound of chicken breast, skinless

- 1/2 cup of mozzarella cheese, in slices or shredded
- For the pesto:
- 1 cup of fresh basil
- 1 clove of garlic (or more if you like garlic)
- 1/4 cup of pine nuts (or cashews)
- 1/3 cup of parmesan cheese
- Salt and pepper to taste (not much more than a dash)
- 1/4 cup of olive oil

Instructions:

Preheat the oven to 350 degrees. Make the pesto by blending all ingredients except for the olive oil in a food processor. Little by little, add the olive oil and blend until smooth.

Place the chicken breast in a greased baking dish and paint 2 to 3 tablespoons of the pesto on top. Bake the chicken, uncovered for 20 minutes. In the last 10 minutes, place the mozzarella cheese on top. This recipe makes one serving plus extra pesto that you can save in the fridge.

Nutrition breakdown:

For the entire recipe of pesto: 853 calories, 86.5g of fat, 14.6g of protein, 10.6g of carbs

For the chicken with two tablespoons of pesto:

667 calories, 29.7g of fat, 92g of protein, 4.7g of carbs

# Keto Ramen with Zucchini Noodles

Ingredients:

- 3 cups of chicken broth
- 2 tablespoons of coconut aminos
- 1 cup of greens of your choice (spinach, arugula, etc.)
- 1 handful of cilantro
- 2 cloves garlic
- 1 small onion, chopped
- 1 tablespoon fresh ginger
- 1/2 cup of mushrooms, sliced
- 1 tablespoon of olive oil
- 1 hard-boiled egg
- 1 cup of zucchini noodles
- Salt, pepper, red pepper flakes to taste

Instructions:

In a medium stock pot, heat the olive oil, garlic, and ginger until fragrant. Add the onions and cook until translucent. Add all other ingredients except the noodles, greens, cilantro, and hard-boiled egg. Bring to a boil and then turn the heat to low and simmer for 30 minutes. Remove from heat before adding the noodles, greens, cilantro and hard-boiled egg, and serve.

If you're making this to bring to work, you can also prepare it by placing all dry ingredients in a mason jar plus half a cube of chicken bouillon instead of chicken stock. Then, add boiling water and cover for 3 to 5 minutes.

Nutrition breakdown:

For one bowl: 318 calories, 21.2g of fat, 15.5g of protein, 19.2g of carbs

# Fajita Bowl

Ingredients:

- 1/2 pound of skirt steak, cut into strips
- 1/2 green bell pepper
- 1/2 red bell pepper
- 1/2 white onion, sliced
- 1 tablespoon of olive oil
- 1/2 head of lettuce of your choice
- 1 handful of cilantro

For the marinade:

- Juice of half a lemon
- Juice of one lime
- 1 clove garlic, minced
- 1 jalapeño, minced (optional)
- 1 teaspoon cumin
- 1 teaspoon of cayenne pepper
- Salt and pepper

Instructions:

Make the marinade by whisking together all ingredients in a small bowl. Allow the skirt steak strips to marinate for 2 to 4 hours or overnight.

In a medium-sized pan, heat the olive oil and cook the steak completely. Remove from heat but don't drain the pan. Add the onions and bell pepper. Cook until they are soft. Serve steak, onions, and bell pepper over the bed of lettuce and top with cilantro.

Nutrition breakdown:

700 calories, 43.8g of fat, 66.9g of protein, 12g of carbs

# DIY Lunchable (Keto-style)

Ingredients:

- 4 slices of deli meat of your choice
- 2 slices of your favorite cheese
- 1/8 cup of crumbled blue cheese or feta cheese
- 2 stalks of celery with 1 tablespoon of almond butter
- 1/4 of a cucumber cut into rounds
- 1/8 cup of blueberries

Don't underestimate how satisfying these simple ingredients can be for lunch on the go. The more variety you can give yourself the better.

Nutrition breakdown:

Lunch with turkey meat, cheddar cheese, feta cheese, celery with almond butter: 470 calories, 33.4g of fat, 34.2g of protein, 9.1g of carbs

Lunch with salami, Gouda cheese, blue cheese, cucumbers, and blueberries: 480 calories, 36g of fat, 31.5g of protein, 8g of carbs

# Dinner Recipes

## Bacon and Kale Hash with a Fried Egg

Ingredients:

- 2 slices of bacon
- 2 cups of kale, cut into ribbons
- 1/2 onion, chopped
- 1/2 cup mushrooms, sliced
- 1 tablespoon olive oil
- 1 egg
- Salt and pepper (and whatever other spices you might like to add - cumin, paprika, etc.)

Instructions:

In a medium-sized pan, heat the olive oil and cook the bacon to your liking. Remove from heat and crumble. Add the mushrooms and onion to the pan and cook until soft. Add in the kale and cook until wilted. Mix the bacon back in and serve with a fried egg on top.

Nutrition breakdown:

432 calories, 38.5g of fat, 14.1g of protein, 8.8g of carbs

# Chicken, Beef, or Lamb Kebabs

Ingredients:

- 1/2 pound of chicken, beef, or lamb cut into bite-sized or 1"
  pieces
- Half of a red onion
- Half of a green bell pepper
- 3 white mushrooms, halved
- 6 wooden skewers (or more, depending on the size you cut
  your ingredients)

For the marinade:

- Juice from 1 lemon
- 2 tablespoons of olive oil
- 1 teaspoon of red wine vinegar
- 1 clove garlic
- A handful of fresh mint
- Salt and Pepper

Instructions:

Whisk together the ingredients for the marinade in a glass bowl.
Place your chicken, beef, or lamb pieces in the marinade. If you're
marinating chicken, I recommend no more than 30 minutes to an
hour. Beef and lamb can marinate for longer, somewhere between 2
and 5 hours.

Prepare the kebabs by alternating meat and vegetables on the wooden skewers. You can spoon whatever leftover marinade you have over the skewers before they cook.

What I like about this recipe is that it's very versatile. You can grill the skewers, cook them on a grill pan, or bake them in the oven. If you're baking, preheat the oven to 400 degrees. You can lay the skewers flat on a cookie sheet lined with aluminum foil, or, if you have a baking dish, you might be able to lay the wooden skewers across so that the meat doesn't touch the bottom. Either way, cook for about 20 to 25 minutes, turning halfway through.

Nutrition breakdown:

With Chicken: 427 calories, 8.5g of fat, 73.2g of protein, 10.5g of carbs

With beef: 396 calories, 13.4g of fat, 48.4g of protein, 10.5g of carbs

With lamb: 436 calories, 21.4g of fat, 48.2g of protein, 10.5g of carbs

Remember, this recipe makes 5 to 6 skewers, so you can divide it into 2 portions.

# Kielbasa and Vegetable Bake

Ingredients:
- 1/2 pound of Kielbasa, cut into rounds

- 1 zucchini, cut into rounds
- Half of a white or yellow onion
- 1/2 cup of cherry tomatoes, cut in half
- 1/2 head of broccoli, cut into small florets
- 2 tablespoons of olive or avocado oil
- 1/4 cup of parmesan cheese
- Salt, pepper, and oregano (or any spice of your choice - thyme, rosemary, etc.)

Instructions:

Preheat the oven to 375. Grease a baking sheet and lay out all ingredients in a single layer. Top with olive or avocado oil and spices.

Bake for 20 to 25 minutes until all vegetables are soft and to your liking. Top with parmesan cheese and serve. This recipe makes two servings.

Nutrition breakdown:

Per serving: 479 calories, 37.3g of fat, 20.7g of protein, 17.3g of carbs

# Stuffed Spaghetti Squash

Ingredients:
- 1 spaghetti squash, cut in half

- 1/4 cup of mozzarella cheese, grated
- 1/4 cup of ricotta cheese, grated
- 2 tablespoons of olive oil, divided

For the meat filling:

- 1/2 pound of ground beef, turkey, or chicken
- 1/2 white onion, chopped
- 2 cloves of garlic
- 2 tablespoons of tomato paste
- 1/2 teaspoon each of dried oregano, parsley, salt and pepper

Instructions:

Preheat the oven to 400 degrees. On a baking sheet, place the squash skin-side down. Drizzle olive oil and salt over the squash and bake for about 45 minutes or until you can easily pierce with a fork. Remove the squash from the oven but don't turn the oven off.

While the squash is cooking, prepare the meat filling by heating the garlic and onion in olive oil. When fragrant, add the meat and cook completely. Add the tomato paste and spices and cook for another minute. Drain and set aside.

When the squash is ready, take it out of the oven and scoop out the insides into a large mixing bowl. Add in the meat mixture and combine. Scoop this mixture back into the empty squash shells and top with cheeses. Return to the oven for another 10 minutes.

This recipe makes quite a lot, so you can divide it into 4 portions.

Nutrition breakdown:

Per servings (4 servings): 396 calories, 31.1g of fat, 16.4g of protein, 14g of carbs

# Collard Greens and Ham

Ingredients:

- 1 bunch of collard greens (about 1/2 pound), with ribs removed and cut into strips
- 2 slices of thick-cut ham, cut into bite-sized pieces
- 2 cloves of garlic
- 2 cups of chicken broth
- 1/2 of a yellow onion
- 1/2 teaspoon each of salt, pepper and red pepper flakes
- 1 tablespoon of olive oil (or as needed. You'll get some fat from the ham)

Instructions:

Cook the ham in a little bit of oil until cooked through. Without draining, add the onion and garlic. If there's a bit of liquid in the pan, add the collard greens directly. If not, add about 1 tablespoon of the chicken broth before adding the collard greens. When the greens start to wilt and sweat, add the rest of the chicken broth and seasonings.

Cook for about 30 minutes more, covered, and then 10 minutes uncovered.

This recipe can be divided into 2 portions.

Nutrition Breakdown:

Per serving: 311 calories, 23.2g of fat, 16g of protein, 11g of carbs

# Keto Chili

Ingredients:

- 1 pound of ground beef or turkey
- 2 cloves of garlic
- 1 onion, chopped
- 1 can of peeled, diced tomatoes, drained
- 1 jalapeño, minced
- 1 cup of beef broth
- 1 tablespoon olive oil
- 1/2 tablespoon each of paprika, salt, pepper, red pepper flakes, chili powder, onion powder, oregano, and cumin (or any combination of flavors you like in your chili)
- 1/4 cup of cheddar cheese, shredded
- 1 tablespoon of sour cream, for serving
- 1 teaspoon chives, chopped, for garnish

Instructions:

In a medium- to large-sized stock pot, heat the olive oil and cook the garlic and jalapeño until fragrant. Add the onion and cook until translucent, about 5 minutes. Add the meat and cook until browned but not completely cooked-through. Add the spices, tomatoes, and 1/8 cup of water and cook for 20 minutes until all of the liquid has evaporated.

Add the beef broth and another 1/8 cup of water. Bring to a boil and then lower the heat to simmer. Cook, uncovered for about 2 hours, stirring occasionally. You may need to add a bit of water every now and again.

This recipe makes 3 to 4 servings. Serve with cheese and a dollop of sour cream.

Nutrition breakdown:

One bowl with turkey: 308 calories, 18.1g of fat, 30.7g of protein, 6.3g of carbs

One bowl with beef: 452 calories, 34.9g of fat, 27.3g of protein, 6.3g of carbs

# Simple Steak and Zucchini

Ingredients:

- 1 6oz steak of your preference
- Salt and pepper

- 1 tablespoon each of fresh thyme and rosemary
- 1 clove of garlic
- 1 tablespoons of olive oil
- 1 zucchini cut into rounds

Instructions:

Preheat the oven to 400 degrees, and pull the steak out of the fridge to come to room temperature. Place zucchini in a greased baking dish with olive oil, salt and pepper. Bake for about 20 minutes. For the steak, preheat a cast-iron skillet on high before adding about a tablespoon of olive oil. When the oil is hot, add the steak and cook for 3 to 4 minutes on each side. Lower the heat and add the garlic and fresh herbs. If you have a cooking brush, pick up some of the liquid and spread it over the top of the steak. Or, you can use a spoon to ladle the liquids in the bottom of the pan over the top. Remove the steak from heat and cover with foil. Allow it to rest for 10 minutes.

Nutrition breakdown:

1127 calories, 47g of fat, 158g of protein, 12.5g of carbs

# Thai Lettuce Wraps

Ingredients:

- 1/2 pound of ground turkey or pork

- 1/2 red onion, chopped
- 1 green onion, chopped
- 1 tablespoon of olive oil
- 1 teaspoon of chili powder
- 1 teaspoon of coconut aminos
- 1 clove garlic, minced
- 1 tablespoon fresh ginger, minced
- Handful of cilantro
- Handful of fresh mint
- Juice from 2 limes
- Red pepper flakes
- Salt and pepper
- 1/8 cup of cashews, chopped
- 4 lettuce leaves

Instructions:

In a medium-sized pan, heat the olive oil with the garlic and ginger. Cook until fragrant and then add the onion. When the onion is translucent, add the ground meat and cook through. Add the lime juice, red pepper flakes, chili powder, salt, pepper, and coconut aminos. Cook for another 5 minutes and then turn off the heat. Mix in the green onions and nuts and combine well.

Serve on the lettuce leaf topped with cilantro and mint.

Nutrition breakdown:

For four lettuce wraps: 723 calories, 51.6g of fat, 45.6g of protein, 26g of carbs

# Simple Lemon Salmon with Asparagus

Ingredients:

- 1 salmon filet, with or without the skin (about 6 ounces)
- One lemon, half juiced, the other sliced thinly
- 1 clove garlic
- 1 teaspoon of garlic powder
- 5 stalks of asparagus
- 1 tablespoon of olive oil
- 1 tablespoon of butter
- Salt and pepper

Instructions:

Preheat the oven to 350 degrees. With a square of aluminum foil, make a boat to put your salmon in. Drizzle a bit of olive oil in the bottom of the boat and lay the salmon in, skin side down if your salmon has the skin. Season the salmon with garlic powder, salt and pepper. Lay the slices of lemon on top and pour the lemon juice over. Pinch the aluminum foil closed over the top of the salmon. Bake for 20 minutes or until the salmon is light pink and flakes easily.

While the salmon is baking, heat the butter and garlic in a medium-sized pan over medium heat. Add the asparagus, salt and pepper and cook to your preferred level of doneness.

Nutrition breakdown:
499 calories, 36g of fat, 36.4g of protein, 8g of carbs

# Bolognese with Zucchini Noodles

Ingredients:
- 1/2 pound of ground pork
- 1/2 pound of ground beef
- 1 tablespoon of butter
- 2 stalks of celery, finely chopped
- 1 onion, finely chopped
- 1/4 cup of whole milk
- 1 can diced, peeled tomatoes
- 3 tablespoons of tomato paste
- 1 tablespoon oregano
- 1 teaspoon nutmeg
- Salt and pepper
- 1 zucchini, spiraled
- Parmesan cheese to serve

Instructions:

In a medium- to large-sized stock pot, melt the butter. Add the celery and onion and cook, stirring frequently, until very soft and translucent, about 10 minutes. Add the ground meat and a bit of salt and cook for 2 minutes. Add the milk and cook until the liquid has evaporated. Add the nutmeg, oregano, salt and pepper. Add in the tomatoes and tomato paste.

Simmer on low heat, uncovered for about 2 hours, adding water if needed. You'll know that it's done when you have a thick and very flavorful sauce.

Serve over zucchini noodles with fresh parmesan cheese. This recipe makes four plates of
Bolognese.

Nutrition breakdown:

For one bowl: 392 calories, 27g of fat, 26.3g of protein, 10.6g of carbs

# Keto Green Bowl with Cauliflower Rice

Ingredients:

- 1/2 head of cauliflower, shredded
- 1/2 chicken breast, skinless and boneless, cut into strips
- 1 cup of spinach, cut into ribbons
- 1 radish, cut into slices

- 1/4 of a zucchini, cut into rounds
- 1/2 avocado
- 1 tablespoon of olive oil
- Salt and pepper

For the chicken marinade:

- 1 teaspoon ginger, ground
- Juice from one lemon
- 1 tablespoon of red wine vinegar
- 1 tablespoon sesame oil
- 1 clove garlic
- Salt and pepper

Instructions:

Whisk together the marinade ingredients and allow the chicken to marinate for 30 minutes to one hour.

Preheat the oven to 350. On a greased backing sheet, lay out the zucchini and chicken in a single layer. Bake for 20 minutes or until the chicken is cooked through.

Meanwhile, cook the cauliflower rice in olive oil in a small- to medium-sized pot until it's to your preferred level of doneness. Turn off the heat but place the spinach on top and cover so that the spinach gets a quick steam.

Assemble the bowl with the cauliflower rice and spinach on the bottom, topped by the chicken and zucchini, radish, avocado, and any seasonings you'd like to add.

Nutrition breakdown:

484 calories, 32.3g of fat, 36.1g of protein, 16.4g of carbs

# Sushi Salad

Ingredients:

- 1/2 head of cauliflower, for rice
- 1/2 can of canned crabmeat
- 2 strips of dried seaweed
- 1/2 cucumber, cut into strips
- 1 radish, sliced
- 1/2 avocado
- 1 tablespoon sesame oil
- 1 tablespoon of mayonnaise
- 1 tablespoon sesame seeds
- 1/4 head of purple cabbage
- 4 ounces of raw, sushi grade salmon or tuna (optional)

Instructions:

Cook the cauliflower rice to your liking. Remove from heat and set aside.

In a medium mixing bowl, combine the crabmeat, sesame oil and mayonnaise. Add the cauliflower rice and raw fish, if you're using it. Serve in a bowl with the seaweed, cabbage, radish slices, avocado, and sesame seeds as garnishes.

This recipe makes two bowls.

Nutrition breakdown:

For one bowl with raw tuna: 380 calories, 26.5g of fat, 20g of protein, 19.3g of carbs

For one bowl with raw salmon: 390 calories, 28.7g of fat, 17.7g of protein, 19.3g of carbs

For one bowl without only crabmeat: 318 calories, 26.2g of fat, 6.1g of protein, 19.3g of carbs

# Simple Roasted Chicken

Ingredients:

- One whole chicken
- Salt and pepper
- 2 sprigs of oregano
- 2 sprigs of thyme
- 2 sprigs of rosemary
- About 4 tablespoons of butter

Instructions:

Preheat the oven to 450 degrees. Prepare the bird by placing it in a deep baking dish or roasting pan. Rub the whole bird outside and in with butter. Add salt and pepper. Place the seasonings inside the cavity.

Bake the bird at 450 for 20 minutes and then lower the heat to 350 for the remainder of the bake. The internal temperature should be 165. Do not cut until you've allowed the chicken to sit for 20 minutes.

Nutrition breakdown:

Now, you're probably not going to eat an entire chicken in one sitting, but you can get about 10 ounces of meat from half of a roasted chicken. With the skin, that breaks down to:

632 calories, 38g of fat, 68g of protein, 0g of carbs

# Eggplant Sandwich

Ingredients:

- 1 medium eggplant, cut into thin slices
- 1/2 cup or 4 slices of mozzarella cheese
- 2 teaspoons of oregano
- 1 tomato, sliced
- 2 slices of deli ham
- 1 egg, whisked
- 4 leaves of arugula (or spinach)
- 2 tablespoons of butter
- 1/2 teaspoon of salt

Instructions:

First, slice and prepare the eggplant by sprinkling with salt and allowing it to dry for 20 minutes.

Assembling the sandwiches can be a bit messy, so make sure you have all of the ingredients easily laid out. You're going to fill the two slices of eggplant with two slices of tomato, 2 slices of mozzarella, slice of ham, oregano and 2 leaves of arugula.

In a medium-sized pan, heat the butter. Before placing your eggplant sandwich in the pan, dip in whisked egg. Fry in the pan for 3 minutes on each side, or until it's nice and brown. You can also broil for a few minutes more to make the sandwiches crispier.

This recipe makes two sandwiches.

Nutrition breakdown:

Per sandwich: 270 calories, 15g of fat, 18.7g of protein, 18.6g of carbs

# Mustard Pork Chops with Broccoli

Ingredients:

- 1 large pork chop, 1 to 2" thick, bone-in
- 1 clove garlic
- 1 tablespoon Dijon mustard
- salt and pepper
- 1/4 cup of fresh parsley, chopped

- 1 tablespoon butter
- 1/4 head of broccoli

Instructions:

In a Ziploc bag, put the mustard, garlic, salt, pepper, and parsley. Mix well and then add the pork chop. Massage the marinade in the pork chop and let sit for 1 to 2 hours.

Preheat the oven to 375 degrees. Place the pork chop with the marinade in a baking dish and bake for 20 to 25 minutes.

While the pork chop is baking, blanch or steam the broccoli. If you're blanching, bring a pot of water with 1 tablespoon of salt to boil. Boil the broccoli for about 4 to 7 minutes until it is to your preferred level of doneness.

Nutrition breakdown:

465 calories, 29.7g of fat, 42.6g of protein, 6.1g of carbs

# Snacks

## Nuts and Berries

1/2 cup of pecans and 1/2 cup of strawberries: 365 calories, 35.8g of fat, 5g of protein, 12.4g of carbs

1/2 cup walnuts and 1/2 cup of blueberries: 425 calories, 38.4g of fat, 9.5g of protein, 18.7g of carbs

As you can see, snacks involving nuts and berries are okay occasionally, but can easily cause you to go over your daily carb limit. Just be mindful of how much you incorporate this snack into your 30-day Keto Challenge.

## Cheese and Deli Meat Rolls

4 slices of deli turkey wrapped up with 4 slices of Monterey jack cheese: 505 calories, 35.3g of fat, 41.8g of protein, 4.3g of carbs

4 slices of low-fat deli ham wrapped up with 4 slices of Swiss cheese: 519 calories, 34.3g of fat, 45.7g of protein, 6.9g of carbs

4 slices of deli chicken wrapped in 4 slices of cheddar: 502 calories, 38.8g of fat, 35.3g of protein, 2.9g of carbs

## Simple Avocado with lime and salt

323 calories, 29.5g of fat, 4g of protein, 17.6g of carbs

# Olives and Cheese

1/4 cup of black olives with 1/4 cup of crumbled blue cheese: 121 calories, 9.8g of fat, 7.2g of protein, .9g of carbs

1/4 cup of green olives with 1/4 cup of feta cheese: 100 calories, 8.1g of fat, 5.3g of protein, 1.6g of carbs

# Deviled-Eggs

Ingredients:
- 2 hard-boiled eggs
- 1 teaspoon Dijon mustard
- 2 tablespoons mayonnaise
- 1/2 teaspoon paprika
- 1/2 teaspoon cayenne pepper or chili pepper
- 1/2 jalapeno, minced (optional)
- salt and pepper
- 2 chives, chopped

Instructions:

While the eggs are boiling, mix the mayonnaise, mustard, paprika, cayenne pepper, salt, pepper, and jalapeño (if using) in a small bowl. When the eggs are done, peel them and cut them in half length-wise. Scoop out the yolks and mix them in the bowl with the other ingredients. When you have a good consistency, scoop the mixture back into the egg whites and top with chives.

Nutrition breakdown:

Without the jalapeño: 353 calories, 31.8g of fat, 13.4g of protein, 2.8g of carbs

With the jalapeño: 355 calories, 31.8g of fat, 13.4g of protein, 3.3g of carbs

## Veggies and Dip

2 stalks of celery and 3 tablespoons of ranch dressing: 195 calories, 20.1g of fat, .8g of protein, 3.6g of carbs

2 stalks of celery and 3 tablespoons of almond butter: 300 calories, 26.7g of fat, 10.3g of protein, 10g of carbs

1/2 cucumber in rounds and 3 tablespoons of blue cheese dressing: 230 calories, 23.2g of fat, 1.2g of protein, 4.3g of carbs

Dark, Dark Chocolate

Let's make this clear - the vast majority of chocolate is not allowed on the Keto diet. And, the vast majority of dark chocolate doesn't make the cut either. But there are a few options out there that you can include as a sweet snack if you're really craving some chocolate. First of all, look for chocolate that is at least 80% cacao. Next, take a look at the carbs. It shouldn't have more than 20g of carbs in a serving.

Even then, if you really want to stay within your daily carb limit, you're not going to want to eat more than about 10g of carbs from this one snack. So be choosy!

# Keto Beef Jerky

Ingredients:

- 1 pound top round beef, boneless and thinly sliced
- 1/8 cup coconut aminos
- 1 teaspoon each of celery powder, onion powder, and cayenne pepper
- 1 clove garlic
- 1 teaspoon of salt
- 1/2 teaspoon red pepper flakes

Instructions:

In a Ziploc bag or small bowl that you can cover with plastic wrap, whisk together the coconut aminos with the garlic and spices (except the salt). Marinade the steak overnight, or at least 4 hours.

When you're ready to cook, preheat the oven to 175 degrees, or whatever your lowest setting is. Line a baking sheet with aluminum foil. The baking sheet is going to sit at the bottom of the oven and catch the drippings. Now, there are a couple of ways that you can cook the jerky in the oven. One way is to hang the jerky over your oven's metal racks. Another is to line them on wooden skewers that will sit across the metal racks. The important thing is that the jerky is able to hang without touching any of the other meat.

Make sure to salt the beef before baking.

Cook for 15 minutes with the door closed to get the temperature up, and then crack the door with a metal or wooden spoon for the remainder of the time. It could take anywhere from 4 to 8 hours for the jerky to reach the right texture.

Nutrition breakdown:
753 calories, 17.8g of fat, 135.3g of protein, 3.9g of carbs

# Bacon-wrapped Asparagus

Ingredients:
- 4 stalks of asparagus
- 4 slices of bacon
- 1/2 tablespoon of olive oil

Instructions:
Preheat the oven to 375 degrees. Drizzle the olive oil in a baking dish. Wrap the single asparagus spears in one slice of bacon and lay it in the dish. Bake for about 25 minutes or until the bacon and asparagus are done to your liking.

Nutrition breakdown:
496 calories, 47.7g of fat, 14.4g of protein, 3.4g of carbs

# Keto Hummus

Ingredients:

- 2 cups of cauliflower, shredded
- 2 tablespoons of olive oil, divided
- 1/2 teaspoon of salt
- 3 cloves of garlic, divided into two portions
- Juice from one lemon
- 2 tablespoons of water
- 1 tablespoon of tahini
- 1 teaspoon paprika
- 1/2 cucumber or 2 celery stalks for serving

Instructions:

In a medium sauce pan, heat one tablespoon of olive oil and half of the garlic until fragrant. Add the cauliflower and water. Cook until soft. With an immersion blender or standing blender, blend the cauliflower with the lemon juice, tahini, salt, paprika, and the remainder of the garlic and olive oil. Add a bit more water if it's very thick.

Serve with sliced cucumbers or celery sticks. This recipe makes 2 servings.

Nutrition breakdown:

Per serving with 1/2 of a cucumber: 218 calories, 18.3g of fat, 4.5g of protein, 12.9g of carbs

Per serving with celery sticks from two stalks: 211 calories, 18.2g of fat, 4.2g of protein, 11.8g of carbs

Taking another look at the recipes

I hope that as you were looking through that long list of recipes, you were able to say to yourself, yeah, I could totally make that. The idea, again, is to provide you with recipes that are easy to recreate as well as delicious so that you can actually enjoy your 30-day Keto Challenge.

So, now that you've gone through the list and picked out the recipes that you want to add to your personal 30-day journey, it's time to actually get everything in writing. In the next chapter, I'll walk you through how to do just that.

# Chapter Three: A 30 Day Template

Now that you've seen the recipes, you can start to fill in your personal 30-day Keto Challenge calendar. Remember, I'm including a template to give you a sense of what your plan might look like, but you should try your best to make it your own.

Before I throw my own 30-day template at you, let's go back to the advice from Chapter One for a moment. Keep these reminders in your head as you go through the creative process of building your 30-day Keto Challenge:

First, remember that you're human. You probably can't devote 100% of your time to this diet. Instead, you need a plan that is going to fit nicely into the life that you already have. That's why the purpose of this guide hasn't been to tell you what to eat but rather to give you the tools to create your own, unique 30-day Keto Diet challenge.

On your calendar, you'll want to write down everything you do during the day so that you can reasonably match the recipes to your schedule. If you feel overwhelmed at the sight of the entire month, break it down into 4 weeks.

The second step is to calculate your daily calorie intake according to the Standard Keto Macro breakdown of 60% fat, 30% protein and

10% carbs. And, don't forget to convert the percentage of calories into grams so that you can easily read nutrition facts. Here are those conversions one more time:

Fat: .60 multiplied by your daily calorie intake, divided by 9

Protein: .30 multiplied by your daily calorie intake, divided by 4

Carbs: .10 multiplied by your daily calorie intake, divided by 4

You should consider intermittent fasting, although it's not a requirement. Remember, if you decide to fast, make sure that you include it strategically in your calendar. For some people, it's better to fast during their busy days because then they won't be thinking about food. For others, that method can be dangerous if they tend to feel dizzy or tired during fasting days. I would recommend that you try both and then adjust your calendar based on how you feel. Keeping yourself well-hydrated is an absolute must. Always have water accessible, and consider writing down the amount of water you drink daily to keep it in your mind.

Of course, even with those tips, it can be helpful to see an example of 30-day challenges. So, with those pieces of advice in mind, take a look at the following templates to see which one motivates you and aligns best with your life.

## The Basic 30-day Keto Challenge

This Keto Challenge is going to be based on a woman between the ages of 21 and 40 who moderately exercise - maybe 3 days a week at the most. She's going to give herself a pretty wide range for daily calories, somewhere between 1700 and 2000 calories. So, her Keto macro breakdown is going to be based on the following:

Calories from fat - 1020 to 1200, or 113g to 133g

Calories from protein - 510 to 600, or 127.5g to 150g

Calories from carbs - 170 to 200, or 42.5g to 50g

## Day one:

Breakfast: Eggs and Bacon (331 calories, 24.6g of fat, 25.2g of protein, 1.2g of carbs)

Snack: Olives and Cheese (121 calories, 9.8g of fat, 7.2g of protein,.9g of carbs)

Lunch: DIY Lunchable (470 calories, 33.4g of fat, 34.2g of protein, 9.1g of carbs)

Snack: Cheese and Deli Ham Rolls (519 calories, 34.3g of fat, 45.7g of protein, 6.9g of carbs)

Dinner: Mustard Pork Chops with Broccoli (465 calories, 29.7g of fat, 42.6g of protein, 6.1g of carbs)

Totals for the day:

1906 calories, 132g of fat, 155g of protein, 24.2g of carbs

## Day two:

Breakfast: Fresh-pressed Green Juice (27 calories, .4g of fat, 1.7g of protein, 4.8g of carbs)

Snack: Bacon-wrapped Asparagus (496 calories, 47.7g of fat, 14.4g of protein, 3.4g of carbs)

Lunch: Keto Tuna on Cucumber Chips (272 calories, 12.3g of fat, 33.7g of protein, 8.4g of carbs)

Snack: Walnuts and Blueberries (425 calories, 38.4g of fat, 9.5g of protein, 18.7g of carbs)

Dinner: Kielbasa and Veggies (479 calories, 37.3g of fat, 20.7g of protein, 17.3g of carbs)

Totals for the day:

1699 calories, 136.1g of fat, 80g of protein, 52.6g of carbs

## Day three:

Breakfast: Cherry Chia Bowl (268 calories, 20.9g of fat, 6.2g of protein, 18.2g of carbs)

Snacks: Deviled-Eggs with jalapeño (355 calories, 31.8g of fat, 13.4g of protein, 3.3g of carbs)

Lunch: Cream of Celery Soup (150 calories, 13.3g of fat, 2.4g of protein, 6.1g of carbs)

Snack: Pecans and Strawberries (365 calories, 35.8g of fat, 5g of protein, 12.4g of carbs)

Dinner: Bolognese with Zucchini Noodles (392 calories, 27g of fat, 26.3g of protein, 10.6g of carbs)

Totals for the day:

1530 calories, 129g of fat, 53.3g of protein, 50.6g of carbs

# Day four:

Breakfast: Mushroom and Spinach Omelet (471 calories, 35.1g of fat, 34.4g of protein, 4.1g of carbs)

Snack: Pecans and Strawberries (365 calories, 35.8g of fat, 5g of protein, 12.4g of carbs)

Lunch: Keto Ramen (318 calories, 21.2g of fat, 15.5g of protein, 19.2g of carbs)

Snack: Keto Hummus with celery (211 calories, 18.2g of fat, 4.2g of protein, 11.8g of carbs)

Dinner: Simple Lemon Salmon with Asparagus (499 calories, 36g of fat, 36.4g of protein, 8g of carbs)

Totals for the day:

1864 calories, 146.3g of fat, 95.5g of protein, 55.5g of carbs

# Day five:

Breakfast: Berry Smoothie (261 calories, 24.3g of fat, 3.1g of protein, 12.5g of carbs)

Lunch: Keto Tuna on Cucumber Chips (272 calories, 12.3g of fat, 33.7g of protein, 8.4g of carbs)

Snack: Keto Beef Jerky (377 calories, 8.9g of fat, 67.7g of protein, 2g of carbs)

Dinner: Thai Lettuce Wraps (723 calories, 51.6g of fat, 45.6g of protein, 26g of carbs)

Totals for the day:

1633 calories, 91.1g of fat, 150.1g of protein, 48.9g of carbs

# Day six:

Breakfast: Scrambled Eggs and Lox (389 calories, 19.9g of fat, 47.7g of protein, 1.3g of carbs)

Lunch: Beef and Cauliflower Rice (470 calories, 33.6g of fat, 31.3g of protein, 15.8g of carbs)

Snack: Bacon-wrapped Asparagus (496 calories, 47.7g of fat, 14.4g of protein, 3.4g of carbs)

Dinner: Keto Green Bowl with Cauliflower Rice (484 calories, 32.3g of fat, 36.1g of protein, 16.4g of carbs)

Totals for the day:

1839 calories, 133.5g of fat, 129.5g of protein, 36.9g of carbs

# Day seven:

Breakfast: Cherry Chia Bowl (268 calories, 20.9g of fat, 6.2g of protein, 18.2g of carbs)

Lunch: Pesto Chicken (667 calories, 29.7g of fat, 92g of protein, 4.7g of carbs)

Snack: Celery and Almond Butter (300 calories, 26.7g of fat, 10.3g of protein, 10g of carbs)

Dinner: Kielbasa and Veggies (479 calories, 37.3g of fat, 20.7g of protein, 17.3g of carbs)

Totals for the day:

1714 calories, 114.6g of fat, 129.2g of protein, 50.2g of carbs

# Day eight:

Breakfast: Keto Toast (103 calories, 9.9g of fat, 3.3g of protein, .5g of carbs)

Snack: Deli turkey and Monterey jack cheese (505 calories, 35.3g of fat, 41.8g of protein, 4.3g of carbs)

Lunch: Super Green Loaded Salad with Raspberry Vinaigrette (325 calories, 26.6g of fat, 6.1g of protein, 20.5g of carbs)

Snack: Black olives and blue cheese (121 calories, 9.8g of fat, 7.2g of protein, .9g of carbs)

Dinner: Stuffed Spaghetti Squash (396 calories, 31.1g of fat, 16.4g of protein, 14g of carbs)

Totals for the day:

1450 calories, 112.7g of fat, 74.8g of protein, 40.2g of carbs

# Day nine:

Breakfast: Keto Eggy Bread (627 calories, 56.4g of fat, 25.1g of protein, 4.9g of carbs)

Lunch: Fajita bowl (700 calories, 43.8g of fat, 66.9g of protein, 12g of carbs)

Dinner: Keto Beef Chili (452 calories, 34.9g of fat, 27.3g of protein, 6.3g of carbs)

Totals for the day:

1779 calories, 135.1g of fat, 119.3g of protein, 23.2g of carbs

## Day ten:

Breakfast: Fresh-pressed Green Juice (27 calories, .4g of fat, 1.7g of protein, 4.8g of carbs)

Snack: Deviled-Eggs without jalapeño (353 calories, 31.8g of fat, 13.4g of protein, 2.8g of carbs)

Lunch: Cauliflower Soup (150 calories, 13.3g of fat, 2.4g of protein, 6.1g of carbs)

Snack: Beef Jerky (753 calories, 17.8g of fat, 135.3g of protein, 3.9g of carbs)

Dinner: Collard Greens and Ham (311 calories, 23.2g of fat, 16g of protein, 11g of carbs)

Totals for the day:

1594 calories, 86.5g of fat, 168.8g of protein, 28.6g of carbs

## Day eleven:

Breakfast: Berry Smoothie (261 calories, 24.3g of fat, 3.1g of protein, 12.5g of carbs)

Snacks: Pecans and Strawberries (365 calories, 35.8g of fat, 5g of protein, 12.4g of carbs)

Lunch: Pesto Chicken (667 calories, 29.7g of fat, 92g of protein, 4.7g of carbs)

Snack: Green Olives and Feta Cheese (100 calories, 8.1g of fat, 5.3g of protein, 1.6g of carbs)

Dinner: Mustard Pork Chops with Broccoli (465 calories, 29.7g of fat, 42.6g of protein, 6.1g of carbs)

Totals for the day:

1858 calories, 127.6g of fat, 56g of protein, 37.3g of carbs

## Day twelve:

Breakfast: Avocado Egg Bake (517 calories, 43.7g of fat, 19.2g of protein, 18g of carbs)

Lunch: DIY Lunchable - turkey option (470 calories, 33.4g of fat, 34.2g of protein, 9.1g of carbs)

Snack: Bacon-wrapped asparagus (496 calories, 47.7g of fat, 14.4g of protein, 3.4g of carbs)

Dinner: Simple Lemon Salmon with Asparagus (499 calories, 36g of fat, 36.4g of protein, 8g of carbs)

Totals for the day:

1982 calories, 160.8g of fat, 104.2g of protein, 38.5g of carbs

## Day thirteen

Breakfast: Eggs and Bacon (331 calories, 24.6g of fat, 25.2g of protein, 1.2g of carbs)

Lunch: Chicken and Broccoli (522 calories, 25.2g of fat, 57.6g of protein, 18g of carbs)

Snack: Avocado with Lime and Salt (323 calories, 29.5g of fat, 4g of protein, 17.6g of carbs)

Dinner: Thai Lettuce Wraps (723 calories, 51.6g of fat, 45.6g of protein, 26g of carbs)

Totals for the day:

1899 calories, 130.9g of fat, 132.4g of protein, 62.8g of carbs

## Day fourteen:

Breakfast: Scrambled Eggs and Lox (389 calories, 19.9g of fat, 47.7g of protein, 1.29g of carbs)

Lunch: Cobb Salad (626 calories, 47.8g of fat, 37.1g of protein, 13.6g of carbs)

Snack: Walnuts and Blueberries (425 calories, 38.4g of fat, 9.5g of protein, 18.7g of carbs)

Dinner: Mustard Pork Chops with Broccoli (465 calories, 29.7g of fat, 42.6g of protein, 6.1g of carbs)

Totals for the day:

1905 calories, 135.8g of fat, 136.9g of protein, 39.7g of carbs

## Day fifteen:

Breakfast: Fresh-pressed green juice (27 calories, .4g of fat,1.7g of protein, 4.8g of carbs)

Snack: Avocado with Lime and Salt (323 calories, 29.5g of fat, 4g of protein, 17.6g of carbs

Lunch: Keto Ramen (318 calories, 21.2g of fat, 15.5g of protein, 19.2g of carbs)

Snack: Deli turkey and Monterey jack cheese (505 calories, 35.3g of fat, 41.8g of protein, 4.3g of carbs)

Dinner: Chicken Kebabs (427 calories, 8.5g of fat, 73.2g of protein, 10.5g of carbs)

Totals for the day:

1600 calories, 94.9g of fat, 136.2g of protein, 56.4g of carbs

# Day sixteen:

Breakfast: Mushroom and Spinach Omelet (471 calories, 35.1g of fat, 34.4g of protein, 4.1g of carbs)

Lunch: Fajita Bowl (700 calories, 43.8g of fat, 66.9g of protein, 12g of carbs)

Snack: Deli chicken and cheddar (502 calories, 38.8g of fat, 35.3g of protein, 2.9g of carbs)

Dinner: Bolognese with Zucchini Noodles (392 calories, 27g of fat, 26.3g of protein, 10.6g of carbs)

Totals for the day:

2065 calories, 144.7g of fat, 162.9g of protein, 29.6g of carbs

# Day seventeen:

Breakfast: Avocado Egg Bake (517 calories, 43.7g of fat, 19.2g of protein, 18g of carbs)

Lunch: Pesto Chicken (667 calories, 29.7g of fat, 92g of protein, 4.7g of carbs)

Snack: Black olives and Blue Cheese (121 calories, 9.8g of fat, 7.2g of protein, .9g of carbs)

Dinner: Keto Green Bowl with Cauliflower Rice (484 calories, 32.3g of fat, 36.1g of protein, 16.4g of carbs)

Totals for the day:

1789 calories, 115.5g of fat, 154.5g of protein, 40g of carbs

## Day eighteen:

Breakfast: Cheesy Scrambled Eggs (394 calories, 30.7g of fat, 26.9g of protein, 1.5g of carbs)

Lunch: DIY Lunchable - salami version (480 calories, 36g of fat, 31.5g of protein, 8g of carbs)

Snack: Beef Jerky (753 calories, 17.8g of fat, 135.3g of protein, 3.9g of carbs)

Dinner: Eggplant Sandwich (270 calories, 15g of fat, 18.7g of protein, 18.6g of carbs)

Totals for the day:

1897 calories, 99.5g of fat, 212.4g of protein, 32g of carbs

## Day nineteen:

Breakfast: Eggs and bacon (331 calories, 24.6g of fat, 25.2g of protein, 1.2g of carbs)

Lunch: Chicken and Broccoli (522 calories, 25.2g of fat, 57.6g of protein, 18g of carbs)

Snack: Pecans and Strawberries (365 calories, 35.8g of fat, 5g of protein, 12.4g of carbs)

Dinner: Keto Turkey Chili (308 calories, 18.1g of fat, 30.7g of protein, 6.3g of carbs)

Totals for the day:

1526 calories, 103.7g of fat, 118.5g of protein, 37.9g of carbs

# Day twenty:

Breakfast: Scrambled Eggs and Lox (389 calories, 19.9g of fat, 47.7g of protein, 1.29g of carbs)

Lunch: Mediterranean Salad (660 calories, 54g of fat, 26.7g of protein, 20.7g of carbs)

Snack: Celery and Ranch (195 calories, 20.1g of fat, .8g of protein, 3.6g of carbs)

Dinner: Simple Roasted Chicken (632 calories, 38g of fat, 68g of protein, 0g of carbs)

Totals for the day:

1876 calories, 132g of fat, 143.2g of protein, 25.6g of carbs

# Day twenty-one:

Breakfast: Keto Toast (103 calories, 9.9g of fat, 3.3g of protein, .5g of carbs)

Snack: Avocado with Lime and Salt (323 calories, 29.5g of fat, 4g of protein, 17.6g of carbs)

Lunch: Brussels Sprouts and Kale Salad (326 calories, 25.3g of fat, 8.9g of protein, 18.9g of carbs)

Snack: Bacon-wrapped Asparagus (496 calories, 47.7g of fat, 14.4g of protein, 3.4g of carbs)

Dinner: Simple Roasted Chicken Leftovers (632 calories, 38g of fat, 68g of protein, 0g of carbs)

Totals for the day:

1880 calories, 150.4g of fat, 98.6g of protein, 40.4g of carbs

# Day twenty-two:

Breakfast: Mushroom and Spinach Omelet (471 calories, 35.1g of fat, 34.4g of protein, 4.1g of carbs)

Lunch: Keto Ramen (318 calories, 21.2g of fat, 15.5g of protein, 19.2g of carbs)

Snack: Beef Jerky (753 calories, 17.8g of fat, 135.3g of protein, 3.9g of carbs)

Dinner: Stuffed Spaghetti Squash (396 calories, 31.1g of fat, 16.4g of protein, 14g of carbs)

Totals for the day:

1938 calories, 105.2g of fat, 201.6g of protein, 41.2g of carbs

# Day twenty-three:

Breakfast: Keto Eggy Bread (627 calories, 56.4g of fat, 25.1g of protein, 4.9g of carbs)

Lunch: Cobb Salad (626 calories, 47.8g of fat, 37.1g of protein, 13.6g of carbs)

Snack: Green Olives and Feta Cheese (100 calories, 8.1g of fat, 5.3g of protein, 1.6g of carbs)

Dinner: Kielbasa and Veggies (479 calories, 37.3g of fat, 20.7g of protein, 17.3g of carbs)

Totals for the day:

1832 calories, 149.6g of fat, 88.2g of protein, 37.4g of carbs

# Day twenty-four:

Breakfast: Fresh-pressed Green Juice (27 calories, .4g of fat, 1.7g of protein, 4.8g of carbs)

Snack: Deviled Eggs with Jalapeño (355 calories, 31.8g of fat, 13.4g of protein, 3.3g of carbs)

Lunch: Garlic Shrimp (622 calories, 47.4g of fat, 47g of protein, 5.2g of carbs)

Snack: Pecans and Strawberries (365 calories, 35.8g of fat, 5g of protein, 12.4g of carbs)

Dinner: Collard Greens and Ham (311 calories, 23.2g of fat, 16g of protein, 11g of carbs)

Totals for the day:

1680 calories, 138.6g of fat, 83.1g of protein, 36.7g of carbs

# Day twenty-five:

Breakfast: Cheesy Scrambled Eggs (394 calories, 30.7g of fat, 26.9g of protein, 1.5g of carbs)

Snacks: Avocado with Lime and Salt (323 calories, 29.5g of fat, 4g of protein, 17.6g of carbs)

Lunch: DIY Lunchable - salami version (480 calories, 36g of fat, 31.5g of protein, 8g of carbs)

Snack: Keto Hummus with Cucumber (218 calories, 18.3g of fat, 4.5g of protein, 12.9g of carbs)

Dinner: Beef Kebabs (396 calories, 13.4g of fat, 48.4g of protein, 10.5g of carbs)

Totals for the day:

1811 calories, 127.9g of fat, 115.3g of protein, 50.5g of carbs

## Day twenty-six:

Breakfast: Berry Smoothie (261 calories, 24.3g of fat, 3.1g of protein, 12.5g of carbs)

Snack: Deviled Eggs without Jalapeño (353 calories, 31.8g of fat, 13.4g of protein, 2.8g of carbs)

Lunch: Cream of Celery Soup (150 calories, 13.3g of fat, 2.4g of protein, 6.1g of carbs)

Snack: Deli Ham with Swiss Cheese (519 calories, 34.3g of fat, 45.7g of protein, 6.9g of carbs)

Dinner: Bacon and Kale Hash with a Fried Egg (432 calories, 38.5g of fat, 14.1g of protein, 8.8g of carbs)

Totals for the day:

1715 calories, 142.2g of fat, 78.7g of protein, 37.1g of carbs

## Day twenty-seven:

Breakfast: Scrambled Eggs and Lox (389 calories, 19.9g of fat, 47.7g of protein, 1.29g of carbs)

Lunch: Keto Meatballs (702 calories, 43.3g of fat, 66.3g of protein, 10.1g of carbs)

Snack: Deli chicken with cheddar (502 calories, 38.8g of fat, 35.3g of protein, 2.9g of carbs)

Dinner: Stuffed Spaghetti Squash (396 calories, 31.1g of fat, 16.4g of protein, 14g of carbs)

Totals for the day:

1989 calories, 133.1g of fat, 165.7g of protein, 28.3g of carbs

## Day twenty-eight:

Breakfast: Cheesy Scrambled Eggs (394 calories, 30.7g of fat, 26.9g of protein, 1.5g of carbs)

Snack: Keto Hummus with Celery (211 calories, 18.2g of fat, 4.2g of protein, 11.8g of carbs)

Lunch: DIY Lunchable - turkey version (470 calories, 33.4g of fat, 34.2g of protein, 9.1g of carbs)

Snack: Walnuts and Blueberries (425 calories, 38.4g of fat, 9.5g of protein, 18.7g of carbs)

Dinner: Collard Greens and Ham (311 calories, 23.2g of fat, 16g of protein, 11g of carbs)

Totals for the day:

1811 calories, 143.9g of fat, 90.8g of protein, 52.1g of carbs

## Day twenty-nine:

Breakfast: Fresh-pressed Green Juice (27 calories, .4g of fat, 1.7g of protein, 4.8g of carbs)

Lunch: Garlic Shrimp (622 calories, 47.4g of fat, 47g of protein, 5.2g of carbs)

Snack: Black Olives and Blue Cheese (121 calories, 9.8g of fat, 7.2g of protein, .9g of carbs)

Dinner: Simple Steak and Zucchini (1127 calories, 47g of fat, 158g of protein, 12.5g of carbs)

Totals for the day:

1897 calories, 104.6g of fat, 213.9g of protein, 23.4g of carbs

## Day thirty:

Breakfast: Mushroom and Spinach Omelet (471 calories, 35.1g of fat, 34.4g of protein, 4.1g of carbs)

Lunch: Cobb Salad (626 calories, 47.8g of fat, 37.1g of protein, 13.6g of carbs)

Snack: Keto Hummus with Cucumber (218 calories, 18.3g of fat, 4.5g of protein, 12.9g of carbs

Dinner: Simple Roasted Chicken (632 calories, 38g of fat, 68g of protein, 0g of carbs)

1947 calories, 139.2g of fat, 144g of protein, 30.6g of carbs

A final word on the template

One thing that I hope you'll take away from the template is that the numbers are not always perfect. Some days the calorie count is high. Some days, you might go over your carb intake by 1 or 2 grams. That's okay. Remember, the calories breakdown is not the most important part of the Keto Diet. Making sure that your body is getting more protein and fat than carbs is the goal.

So, as you're going through the template and making it your own, keep that in mind. Every day is never going to be perfectly 1900 calories with 127g of fat and 48g of carbs. But as much as you can land around those numbers, you're in good shape.

# Conclusion

By this point, you're at an exciting stage in the process of your 30-Day Keto Diet Challenge. Maybe you've created your calendar or are ready to get started. Maybe you haven't done any of the actual planning but you're feeling inspired after reading through the different recipes.

No matter where you are in your journey, take a moment to show yourself a bit of gratitude. You're taking a big step, and you've shown just how strong and dedicated you are by picking up this guide and getting started.

Before I send you on your way, let's review some of the important highlights you found in this guide. Allow them to inspire you as you move forward in your 30-day challenge.

Set yourself up for success with a bit of organization. A calendar, a visual guide, whatever you need to see your month laid out will be helpful and motivating

Find your unique calorie intake, but don't get bogged down in the math. Everyone approaches the Keto Diet slightly differently, so find the path that works best for you, whether that means counting every calorie or not paying too much attention to numbers. You'll burn fat either way.

Take care of yourself. Drink water. Find the people who will support you. Decide whether fasting is the right approach to dieting or not. You are the only one on this journey, so make sure that you pack only what you need and what will make you feel good. Your health is the highest priority

So get out there! Find your recipes, find your style, and start the transition to ketosis!